SUNLIGHT

STRIPPING

SHADOWS

BARE

SUNLIGHT

STRIPPING

SHADOWS

BARE

AMY. B. GARRATT

Sunlight Stripping Shadows Bare
First published in Great Britain in 2021 by:
DAISA PUBLISHING
An imprint of PARTNERSHIP PUBLISHING

Written by Amy.B.Garratt
Copyright © Amy.B.Garratt

A CIP catalogue record for this book is available from the British Library.

Paperback ISBN 978-1-8384243-2-9

Book cover design by: Partnership Publishing
Book Cover Images ©Shutterstock 1903428238, 740325295, 1166238973
Internal Images ©Shutterstock 1202345491, 1221466057, 1457714681, 1754956040, 1898592469

Book typeset by:
PARTNERSHIP PUBLISHING
Barton upon Humber
North Lincolnshire
United Kingdom
DN18 5RG

www.partnershippublishing.co.uk

Printed in England

Partnership Publishing is committed to a sustainable future for our business, our readers and our planet. This book is made from paper certified by the Forestry Stewardship Council (FSC), an organisation dedicated to promoting responsible management of forest resources.

For Jamie, Lily and Phoebe,
my greatest adventure and loves.

In loving memory of my Grandad Sid Bidmead.

My poems are the rambles and scrambles of
my own head and heart.

contents

breaking

healing

imagining

loving

growing

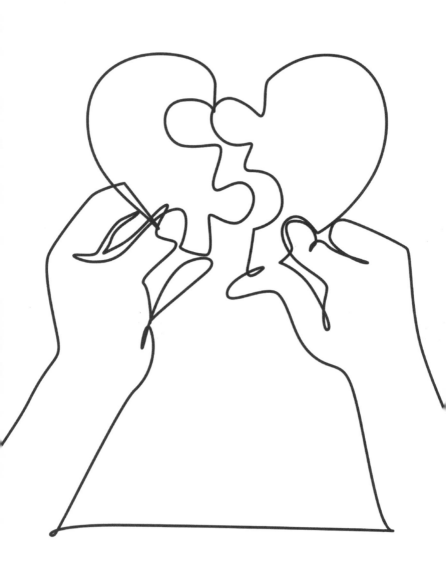

breaking

'Trust mixed with lust is easily broken.'

- a piece of the puzzle

Torn and no longer needed.

The lies are scattered all around me.

I try to make the edges fit together, a complete jigsaw
so I can picture why you have done this. It gives me no
comfort to see it consolidating.

A bleak outlook that none of my actions affected the
decisions you came to. You slipped into the dark, under
other sheets, while mine lie cold.

Unruffled, unsliced, unsleeping.

Rebuffed, diced, weeping...

- summer romance

The sad love songs strike me the hardest, the aching joyful blow, of love found and love lost, the topcoat of a summer songs glow. Those brief and beautiful romances, played out under hottest sun, burn the brightest and the quickest, as loves flames comes all undone. As the clock hands slip forward, summer time skips along. The new day dawns more quickly, as the new love has all gone.

- amen to the formerly beloved

Our love lies here dead... that must be why you haunted me.

I knelt and heard all the old lessons repeated back to me.

Whispered promises in the dark... broken by the daybreak... repeated lies that the sun would never rise unless you allowed it to.

The visits to our past have stopped... the wreath I laid is bare, withered and torn. Scripture unquoted and unrehearsed.

Our obituary is cliche.

One chose faith, one chose infidelity.

Never in sync with the same side of that monogamous currency...

I spent my coins and hours in bars to forget.
Illuminated hymns of rock and distain, distant from my
true self and my old purpose.

An angel woke me from my uneasy slumber.
I bathed myself in the altar of redemption... and I rose
again, anew.

Exorcised the past, to cross into the future.
In the name of the truth, the beauty and the love.

Amen.

- heartbreak

Stop apologising. For having the nerve to feel, the
audacity to collect all your broken parts and splice
them into a mosaic of a respectable human being. You
are a work of art. Pain crafted into something pure.

- 'proseology'

An apology only really benefits the person who's giving it. They can then say they gave it.

The other person doesn't have to accept it, especially if it doesn't compensate for their feelings about how they've been treated.

Apologies are an unburdening.

Sincere or not, the cause of the hurt and the reason for the apology can still lie between you.

Like... shredding non-reusable wrapping paper, binned the moment it's deemed unnecessary.

I'm sorry YOU feel/felt that way-the trickster of apologies.

You are blaming the person who feels slighted, because it is their own fault they are hurting.

Their feelings have caused the hurt, and not the apologiser... or their actions.

It is a limited act of contrition...

- hard to handle

When I overdose on well-wishes, my mind lashes out. It doesn't want to believe in good intentions. Good intentions have never gotten me very far, and always come crashing down. I'm held together by the layers of all my flaws, and embroidered with the accusations of everything that's wrong with me. I am hard to handle, porcelain expected to take beatings like rocks on a stormy shoreline. I am the climbing ivy vine, searching for a vertical hold but without sturdy consistent support. I am the ache and the fever, of sweating out the poisoned page... I am the consequence of mistakes.

- porcelain

Fresh- faced, powdered grace... propped up among the dolls and lace. Fragile porcelain expressions, of daily inwards obsessions. To dance with a poet, is to be immortal. They trace every curve of your mind, cement you in place and in time. Echoing words make room for peace, in a labyrinth of endless locked doors. When your portrait hangs in the eternal gallery, you can pay for the pleasure of an audience... cover the door charge of your personal hell and own devils dowry.

- goodbyes

The tale goes, that it's one for sorrow and two for joy. As we soar through life together as a pair of magpies, floating through clouds until the moment when time inevitably pulls us apart... the sorrow is born from becoming one again.

We lie alone in our nest, a brittle bed of pine cones and memories, tearing our skin on the edges of the sharp absence of warmth that joy occupied. The jewelled hand is empty of a neighbouring palm, and the lace hanging at the curtain shields from an empty sight of the paused world beyond.

The weight of grief pools at our neck, threatening to drag us under with wave after wave of endless shores to walk along. The thing about goodbyes, is that we have no choice in them. Yet we choose the final sorrow, because we yearn for the daily joy we will receive.

- density

Hollow sounds in an aching chest,
Thoughts tangled in scattered heartbeats,
A cats cradle created of empty desires.

Webs stretched and constructed delicately.
Optimism is a mask slipped on,
Underneath lies cracks and sores.

A stolen face of outward expression,
Imperfections intricately painted gold.
Shattered jigsaw pieces hiding density.

- love sick

Love sick, with pages torn.
Lonely, filled with bitter scorn.
Languish, as I begin to mourn.
Lethargic, with much forlorn.

Lowly, this toil has left me worn...
Lost, my soul has withdrawn.
Ludicrous, since I was forewarned.
Forsaken... by a pricking thorn.

- second skin

I needed someone to love me with my clothes on.

When the music had finished throbbing overhead.

When the sun came up and highlighted my cheeks of smudged mascara.

Spare me of regret.

The regrettable act of confiding all my darkness to you.

Acceptance is desired as much as sensation.

Write my future.

In digits, or cursive, or spoken softly into an earpiece.

Take note of my artifice, I wear this confidence like a second skin and shed it behind a locked door.

- you

Do you see it? The collective, 'you'.
This made-up band of characters, who I consistently smash my emotions to pieces for.

These 'people' in turn, who I would crawl over broken shards to help, and tear my own wants and needs to ribbons... making myself secondary in a drawn out process.

Would they notice if I fell into my own shadow, and blended into this image they have made of me?
I imagine not... as fiction doesn't often bother with fact after all.

This caricature of a person, doesn't exist.
I am weak and folded onto myself... into myself, like a twisted paper crane.

I am crooked, and small, but dependable.
Crying out for acknowledgement, for justice, for closure.

- ladies room confessions

We sit and scroll, wondering why they haven't text back. Missed calls ignite our frustration. We down our cheap drink to work up the courage to leave the cubicle and go back out there. Stalking the plains of flashing lights. Summoning strength to stand side by side with these confident creatures, people completely out of our league. Physically, emotionally, spiritually, they all seem to be "more" while we try to pale into the shape of the wall next to the dance floor. They grind up against each other while we grind our teeth in anguish, a socially awkward animal trapped in a cage of social conventions. Seated on the safety of the bowl, we reapply our lipstick, we take a deep breath, we lip sync along to the distant music. Hear the rambles of the intoxicated, "OMG babe don't cry, he's just... he has no idea. I mean... I know I just met you 30 seconds ago, but you seem SO great!" Our ladies room confessions lay amongst a hive of gossip or in a sanctuary for betrayed souls.

- I had a childish fantasy

Sew up my eyes with the lies you sold me,
Give me one last bitter taste of air.
Let my mind unwind, as my life unravels...
That's really all that I can bear.

I fell for every stupid line,
like a puppet on a string.
Given the gift of a broken soul,
making this my everything.

Solitude feels so raw,
Now the fairytale's at an end...
I'm not a princess to adore,
And now I cant even pretend.

When I fell through the looking glass,
There was no wonderland.
Shattered broken faces,
And full of deceit... so bland.

It turns out the slipper doesn't fit,

And there is no ball.

Life is not a simple thing,

there's no happily ever after... at all.

- practical magic

Brokenness, fragile, brittle, battered.

Emotions lay scattered amongst our old love letters.

We were doomed from the start, and yet I always held out in the hope that I was wrong.

The curse wouldn't play a part in our love story, and I wasn't meant to live with a broken heart. No cures, no quick fixes, no words of comfort from the Grimoire on the table... which may as well be empty, as no answers lie in it for me.

The potions have all gone stale, my head is weak and I crawl into myself and try to find the peace I had before... amongst all of my broken pieces on the hollow distant floor...

- they say...

'The problem is... she's just too sensitive. She takes too much to heart, so easily offended, so quick to be hurt and make us all feel bad'.

I've worn insults like a second skin for the past two decades. I am patches of experience sewn together neatly over unhealed wounds. The nerves exposed to oxygen, the sinew underneath raw from all the words and bruises I've been bombarded with. I am too fragile, too anxious, too this or too that... for people who are unscathed, unaffected, unable to see past their own life decisions.

If I am too much... why don't you look to the narcissists who made me this way... the unloving, the unsympathetic, the untrustworthy... who carved all my insecurities upon the tablet of stone I carry in my chest day after day... then maybe my sensitivity won't come as such a shock to you?

- scars

Drowning in self importance.

Memories of when you had something more.

Stained glass bleeds your name, this pain we both bore.

Spelling out the quiet tragedy.

This loss of innocence.

Pretending that scars fade, these red lines your penance.

Shining silver magnet.

This thin piece of steel.

Attracted to the other, so it cannot heal.

Watching this reflection.

Marked by blackened rain.

Falling from your eyes, and crying out in vain.

Hidden tears, carry on this pantomime.

Lift the marked head, now repeat...

'everything's just fine'.

- emotional dysfunction

Coiled emotional dysfunction.

I try to attach a name to what is inside.

I vary between extremes, barely able to keep up with myself.

I'm walking on air, then choking as sweet air turns bitter in my mouth.

I wonder where I went so wrong...

Useless daughter, vicious lover, bitter friend.

Tragic beautiful words, desperate to be written...

Yet they'll never understand, and don't promise what you cant keep.

I'm sick of comparing myself to my counterparts... I want to be happy with the living.

- lessons

Aching inner peace. Moments of stolen ecstasy and temporary solace... I am a pupil at the school of gaslighting. Painfully apologetic for all the things you've done to me... due to the interpretation of my behaviour.

You were never like this before I came along. I have created you. My face has unlocked the door to your darkest tendencies and lack of discipline. A broken man with empty promises to change.

- house of cards

Destiny seemed like something constantly escaping
my grasp. Fate was not laid out before me, it was like
a house of cards. Poorly built and fragile to fall to
nothingness. Seeking hearts but only ever receiving
clubs in response. Red or black, passion or blank
thought... play your hand.

- the performer

I don't know where he's been... but neither does she. The skin he has touched, the sights he has seen. The mask he carefully kept in it's place, the crows look of guilt all over his face.

Scrubs his hands clean of the scent of the dead, and the waft of perfume that comes out of my bed. The perfect performance of guilt, acted with skill. He opens his arms, to forget the plagues chill.

- grounded

The memories come to me when I least expect. A piece of music, a turn of phrase. Then I'm transported... oh how we fought. For your attention, for your need to deceive me. The portrayal of me... your discarded muse. I'm not allowed to leave, yet you won't stay indoors. I'm trapped... in this hell lined with all my rivals. I'm painted as a villain, when you are the one who breaks all contracts. I stand under hot scalding water, the current of souls swirling down a vacant drain... my florid flesh aches for release. Then I remember you are gone, and I escaped. I take in a deep rattled breath to ground my feet to the present.

- a popular myth...

You cannot have pleasure without pain. Pleasure is only exquisite when it's carved into your skin, a scalding longing, an aching wound to nurse. The theories of pleasure seem to align with this idea that you must suffer to be worthy of having it.

No pain, no gain. You can appreciate sunshine after a storm... but you can also bask in it and wonder at its beauty every day you open your eyes to see it. The pursuit of pleasure is in tiny details, not in the land of despair and misery as a reward for the scars we bare.

- pain

Pain has a curved chiselled edge of memory when you look into the past. Pain in the present is a cruel and breath stealing miserable existence. Pain in the future is fear, fear of an unfulfilled wish.

- your memory

How can I hold a memory in my hand... I look at your photographs, and try to soothe my pain with the glossy images. Hoping to be subdued by ghosts captured in the past. Nothing can explain the empty space that your love used to occupy, the unplayed music that was always a favourite, when words ache through lyrics that seemed written just for you. The hours are now drawn out longer than the minutes we ever spent together, and I await her kiss... tangled with strings of fate.

-

- anatomy

What is it you need?

Something solid to claim fame to?

You are the first of your kind, an endangered anatomy. I trace the outline of your skin so I can remember it when you have gone from me. No matter how much adoration I lay at your altar, you still seek more from strangers. I am the gatekeeper, and you always escape.

- grief

The only time I think of you, is when my heart beats.
When my breath catches, in the fog of my brain.
During the sun rise, the daylight hours of clouds
dancing far above me... I remember your name.

The twilight, as the paint work framing our globe
bleeds into itself... the darkness comes and pin pricks
of a distant life spring forth.

As I hear running water, a symphony of swirling
and crashing and sudden stillness. Tiny fragments
of glass that I trace your memory into and build
unconquerable castles with.

Dreams bombarded with frozen images and an
eagerness to contain them into a keepsake.

Yes... the only time I think of you,
is when my eyes open or close...
and when my heart beats.

- ashes

We're told to change the narrative. Change our perspective on things. Assign new memories to the traumatic old ones which keep us up at night. Instead I chose to change the scenery, leave the lights and noise and chaotic streets I'd grown so accustomed to. I painted a new backdrop with all the hues I wanted to see every day. The canvas was fresh, the entrances and exits unused, the dialogue dynamic and honest. No repetition of the same arguments, the same journeys with no conclusive destination in mind. I lit a match on the past, began fanning the flames of city heartache... and burnt it all to the ground while I stood watch over the ashes.

- letting you go

I had to let you go. The pain it bore me to carry you onto my next life would be too much for my hands to hold. Memories steeped into your pages, the swirls and loops I could never bring myself to look upon again. I tore you apart and burnt all the mistakes and embarrassment and confessions I'd laid within. I wanted to erase the idea of ever knowing you. To know and be known is a dangerous game to play with someone who won't play by the rules, and I have the scars to prove it.

Rest in peace... or I will have none.

- brokenness

"My narrative is often rooted in loss of 'self'. I lost myself in relationships, in desperation for love which led to abuse... of my trust, my emotions and physically. Loss of friendships and connections, loss of my personality due to lack of concentration/confidence/ability to focus, loss of my carefree side to anxiety and pessimism. I often gravitate to brokenness because I understand it more than feeling whole."

healing

'Sticks and stones broke my sweet spirit.'

8am

Stop

9am

Being

10am

So

11am

Hard

12 noon

On

1pm

Yourself

2pm

(Tea and Biscuits)

3pm
Give

4pm
Yourself

5pm
A

6pm
Break

7pm
Beautiful

8pm
Human

———————

- beauty

Subjective, crushing, lovely all at once.
A sunset, a muse, music flowing through.

An intake of breath, a glance, a stare.
Wafting of perfume through stormy air.

- affirmation

Think positive, focus on the good, make peace,
be better, be happy, let the sadness cease.

Pour another measure, of those jolly drinking
affirmations. Take a shot at a brand new shiny
personality creation.

The slow spread of warmth through your chest; begins
as a slow burn... the life you want to change,
for the life you yearn.

1. Hot beverage.

Tea, coffee, hot chocolate, chai, fruit, mulled wine if serious. Can substitute for a comforting cold drink such as milk... or a further bottle of wine if inspiration won't come.

2. An hour long bath.

Bath bombs, bath salts, bubbles, rose petals... that start to get in your way so you have to pick them out again. Quiet.... or trashy music. A shower has a similar affect, as the water drums into your skull/soul while you contemplate the world.

3. Walk.

Observe nature, the leaves, flowers, trees. Get distracted trying to get a good insta picture and forget what you meant to write in the first place!

4. Talk.

People watch. Witness life happen. Or curl up under a duvet, have a cry, and then pull out your notebook again at a later date.

P.S When I started this list I had no idea what to write!

- mindfulness

When my restless heart wanders, I try to meditate. Clearing my mind is not an easy task, instead I try to imagine what calm would look like. Something soft, something sturdy, something I can grasp in my hands and keep safe next to my beating chest. I don't want to imagine beauty. I want to live in it. I want to swim in it, soak it into my pores and breathe it in. I want to open my eyes to it, and ache to stay awake because I don't want to miss a moment of it's painful exquisite experience. I don't want to play pretend, I want to play dress up and adorn myself in all the beautiful robes that this world has to offer.

- ambivert

She's the life of the party... as long as it's on her own terms. She can hold her own... but might have to be picked up off the floor. She likes to spontaneously make meticulous plans and trace back every conversation you've had. Social anxiety is an issue, but she'll also be drawn into a conversation with a stranger nursing a pint of bitter. Her laugh is contagious, especially during inappropriate moments. She is loyal, to her friends and her duvet days, and walks through life like a lioness. Protective, and hunting for the next moment. If she's quiet, she's curled up with a good book, or a pile of intrusive thoughts. She's loving, considerate but careful.

- autumn girl

Sweet girl, you radiate like sunbeams.

Delicate, sharp, filtering through a leafy canopy to illuminate the world around you.

Soft, sharp edges rounded... and welcoming.

Like a woollen blanket on a crisp cool morning.

Dewdrops resting on flushed cheeks.

- my blank canvas

A collection of intrusive thoughts and deep-set emotions. Chaotic, abrupt and gentle at once. The words burst forth from me, without planning. I endeavour to always be honest, whether painful or happy. I paint a mental canvas with all my life experience, and the extra details are added in through walks in nature and people watching. I observe a rose and a stranger drinking coffee in the same calculating manner. I imagine their lives and twisted roots and the reason behind the blend of coffee, or brand of compost. I try to not feel shame and self-edit too much, or the 'real' aspect of my writing is lost in translation. My poetry inevitably has a sadness behind it, because I can more easily understand broken things than wholeness...

- solitude

It can reawaken long forgotten passions. If you allow your mind to be still, away from constant chatter and distractions. You also open the door to create new potential experiences.

It can unlock all the terrors of your mind, and lay them bare. Like an emotional air dry on a warm day. You can formulate plans... or just release a build up of years of hidden tears.

It can open you up to an emotional kaleidoscope of thoughts you never normally dwell on. Bring about solutions you never would have had the time to construct.

It can give you the gift of beauty with clarity. A walk through the woodland with only the company of the leaves and birds and clouds, can give you true contentment. Loving time with just yourself, is true self-care and deep appreciation.

- types

I'm the type of mother, who always second guesses herself. Her abilities, the abilities you are just magically supposed to have with no real "on the job" training. Thrown in the deep end and learning how to swim alongside this tiny human who looks to you for guidance.

I'm the type of poet, who struggles with form and precise methods. I try to make things rhyme, but I don't always have the time... I often feel like my words are just tumbling out of my brain, with no poetic content at all.

I'm the type of lover, who always wants to be praised for doing the right thing. I'm screaming inside but I'm "so strong, so selfless, so kind, so caring, so nice..." and I need those brownie points to feel at all adequate.

I'm the type of friend, who feels friendless. I accept the idea that I'm a massive burden, and try not to bother anyone with my melancholy. Whilst simultaneously getting stressed out about plans that I swore I wasn't going to get stressed about making.

- tell me...

Tell me.

Tell me how to relate.

Tell me how to help you feel.

Tell me how I can stop the rush.

The onslaught of rabid emotions.

Tidal waves of thoughts, crashing and turning

on themselves. Brutal and foaming at the mouth.

Endless swirling and clinging onto the small islands

surrounding this dark abyss.

Just tell me what the matter is.

Just tell me how to help you.

Just tell me what to do.

Tell me.

- consciousness

The moment when you wake, where you still don't exist quite yet. No memories, no existence outside of softness and breathing. Before the click of your consciousness coming back on, in the distant land somewhere between mirror talk and breakfast, is the joy of a blank slate. Being completely free of obligations or concern, a brief moment of true mindfulness and one select grounded beautiful snapshot of simply living.

Fresh air.

If possible a nice walk in nature, preferably through some woods and lots of greenery. Flowers are good too.

Books.

Endless far off worlds, characters, scenarios, to distract my anxiety from reality as much as possible.

Music.

Playlists of varying lengths, genres, moods and artists. Diversity.

Trashy films.

Sometimes a little of what you fancy goes a long way, even if the plot is predictable (see-Hallmark Christmas films!)

Unexpected hobbies.

Learning keeps the mind sharp and fixed. And stops you scrolling endlessly too!

'Do not disturb' phone mode.

Give your emotions a break.

Cliche.

But... herbal remedies, lots of water, sometimes some medicinal help.

Talking, writing, singing, playing.

These can all give your mind a boost.

Love.

Wherever you can find it. A warming sight, a cuddle with a pet, chatting to friends and family.

Kisses, hugs, sexy encounters.

Encouraging words.

- truth to power

2018

I recently read "it all begins and ends in your mind. What you give power to, has power over you."
So this is how it all begins. I feel betrayed by my own mind, and ashamed of my companion, depression.

Many of the relationships I've formed in my life rely on self deprecating humour. At gatherings we distract one another with jokes, and often you need that relief to be able to carry on with the day to day tasks. Seeking emotional support is not so simple when you can't form the words to explain, or you hear, "what does she have to be upset about... just try harder."

Some days I can manage to be productive and upbeat. Others it takes me 5 hours to convince myself to bathe. I recently spent 3 days in the house before I realised I hadn't ventured beyond the front door. Now, if I had a broken leg, no-one would tell me to walk it off, but an illness of the brain is easily dismissed as "not trying."

Depression becomes the elephant in the room, the observer waiting for the opportune moment to strike. Painful, and intrusive thoughts are common place. There's no rhyme or reason to them. I can feel desperately lonely, painfully sad, furious or panicked. It gives me a metaphorical kick in the ribs. Followed by a chorus line of "you are worthless."

I re-live all the painful experiences I wish I could forget, with far too much clarity. And all of my faults, listed as bullet points as reasons to despise me, by people I had called friends. The experience of meeting me is watching a battle between the need for acceptance and panic. The desire to not be hurt, instead of let anyone else in and repeat the process. Depression reminds me it should come as no surprise to anyone that I'm awful.

The gut wrenching feeling I had ruined someone others described so fondly. He'd never been a compulsive liar or cheat before I came along. He'd never gotten physical and harmed anyone else, that was a kind of special bond between us. Nobody else would put up with my shit like he would, I asked too many questions and bruised too easily.

I toasted to the lives of dearly departed loved ones and those struggling through illnesses of their own, attempting to cry myself to sleep but being denied any respite. Started a career tending to others needs, yet not knowing how to tend to my own.

But I persevered, helped along by meeting the love of my life, forming a closer family bond and those friends who'd stuck beside me. We created new positive experiences. My mind felt manageable. Like an allergy you keep an eye on, or the first day after the flu, still feeling delicate but able to function.

Then I began to see the outline of depression lurking in the doorway of my new life. Like the ex-partner dropping in for a chat you didn't ask for. I knew something had to be done.

So here's how it ends... or starts. I asked for professional help. And I applied to this open discussion, some paragraphs emailed on a whim. In the hope that this cathartic experience would clear out my cobwebs, the boxes in the attic of my past finally sorted through.

I know this is no magical cure, I still have a journey to make, but I'm no longer keeping it a secret. Depression may be the longest relationship I've ever had, it's always made sure to keep in touch, but I'm no longer taking it's calls.

imagining

'Playground summer rules, treated like fools.
Seeking validation, from our imagination.'

- the wanderer

The idyllic land of nymphs is where my heart wanders. Over hills, and trees, and shaded forest. The beauty, the peace, the great wide open world longing for exploration.

But tread carefully... do not bend a blade of grass, break a branch, steal the oceans breath or capture that which should be free. Be kind to our mother, our sister, our cousin.

Cherish her spirit, her broad and silent heartbeat. Care for her, or she will unleash fire upon us all. Be gentle, or suffer the nymphs wrath for betraying all they hold dear.

- the faerie door

Stretching up toward the sun, the yellow beams uncurl the days fresh thoughts. Woodland home awakens and sweet mist clearing.

They will leave a subtle sparkle in their wake, for the wisest travellers to follow.

Retracing their swift journey, slowly threading a pathway back to the secret faerie door... and fae world beyond.

- gemini

I'm never on time. Either exceptionally early or ridiculously late and flustered. Procrastinating and hyper focused activities are the two sides of my gemini induced coin. I cannot move or I cannot be moved by anything or anyone if the mood takes me this way or that. I am open but cautious, an open door with a screen between the threshold and the garden. Impulsive decisions scrawled across a carefully planned journal of weekly activities. An old favourite next to a never seen before dramatic monologue. I sleep at the dawning and stare into the velvet cake sky. You must accept my contradictory statements to see what my spirit is truly made from...

- change

Unhurried stares...
On the sodden leaf strewn path,
I look to the sky.

Through the crimson loft...
Daylight drifts to us below.
Cradles me in love.

The land in between...
Growing leaf and the fallen.
I breathe in change.

- the witches

Witches familiar, slinky black coat and prowling through midnight gardens. We stalk, for fun, for mischief, for play.

We guard our coven, with our smoky form. Sharpen our claws, and in each of our nine lives, we are reborn... sworn into cunning.

When shall we three meet again?
There's some magic to be done.
Spells to conjure, potions to make,
Cooking and boiling and brewing and bake.

Thrice' round the cauldron, we stir stir stir.
Night black as the cat, who watches our work.
The power of nature, the wind and the tree.
The coven of merry mirth and much glee.

- the goblin king

I'll tell you a tale of the goblin king. As tall as a tower, and right arm full of swing. He bashed his way through homes and through towns, the most fierce warrior from all around. The pixies did fear him (a few hobbits did too), but his one tiny secret, no-one really knew.

He always disappeared, on a full moon night, some started to suspect "is he a werewolf out of sight?" The truth however, was much more simple. Like the impulse of a bird flying north on it's wing. He wanted to hide... his urges to sing! He bellowed, and bleated, and roared at the night. He shouted and spluttered, with all of his might. And when morning broke, he wiped his large brow, returned to his kingdom... where we all must bow.

- the furies

We, the erinyes, stand before you.

We know what you have done, and we seek atonement.

The justice, the truth of all the things you hide in the dark. We are the darkness, born from it, born from blood and cruelty, and we bring your deeds into the light.

The cost of your words is not forgiveness, we have not that power. It is vengeance, and retribution for those you have defiled. The words from your lips cast poison into our world, and murdered innocence.

Our wrath, our curse upon you, is laid from your victims cries. We are sisters, maidens, we come to hunt you down... and lay you low.

- before you sleep

Swish that wand,
And turn three times.
Click your heels,
Then wish a goodnight.

Gratitude for our nature,
And gratitude for the home.
Happiness for all living,
and for those all alone.

Silver as moonlight,
keep a coin by the bed.
Turn it over thrice,
to rest a weary head.

-emotionally distant pumpkin

It's not you, it's me.

I just need to grow... and be free.

Got to live for myself, not just for thee.

I can't just paint a smile on my face.

The truth is... I need my own space.

Just got to live at my own pace.

You want me to glow from the inside.

Yet all I want to do is hide,

from this festivity I just cannot abide.

It's really not you, it's all about me.

My skin deep issues bring no glee,

so I plea... leave me here to be.

- mood ring

Watch out for the kaleidoscope of colours. They'll turn your head the full 360. All your hair stands on end, and skin begins to itch. Look down at that ring you found in the thrift store... yet you've never seen it glow that way before.

A murky dirty grey... with no explanations or instructions what to say. Green means jealousy, yellow is confusion, pink is innocence, purple is mystical illusion (at least that's what you assume as you've never seen it happen). But whenever it's grey, you feel stuck in this repeating pattern.

Red is for love, or is red for passion? Black is vague, or is 'moody' just in fashion? Grey leaves your mouth feeling stuck and like a puppet on a string... can you use a ring for voodoo, or is that not the 'done' thing...

- grimoire of instagram

How to conjure more followers.

- Entice them into your web of likes.

- Create an amulet of protection from trolls.

- Summon positive feedback and energy.

- Come up with a classy rune.

- Construct your own talisman so you are easily recognisable.

- Ooze charm and divination.

- Deities vs Demons:
  Who is your content really reaching?

- Sorcery 101 (2020-404)

- the three sisters

Once upon a time, there were three sisters. One was wise, one was cruel and one was kind. They frolicked through the forest, past mushrooms and wet earth, fallen broken leaves and branches... until they came across an injured deer. It lay before them, but life coursed through it still. The wise sister thought they should leave it be, let nature take its course and claim another October soul. The cruel sister thought they should benefit from putting it out of its own misery, and use it for meat and pelt. But the kind sister offered to sit with it, and give it comfort until it went on it's way to the next world. The cruel sister tutted, while the wise sister nodded and continued on her way. The kind sister held the deers head, and cried a silent tear for its spirit. She returned home to find the house empty... her sisters had fallen into a deep dark hole and would never return. Nature had cruelly had its way with them and kindness had prevented the youngest from a horrible fate.

- what's your tipple?

What's your tipple? Drink of choice?
Something smooth? Makes you raise your voice?

What's your poison? Secret shame?
What's the drink, on which you always place the blame?

What's that chill? Is it just the ice?
Runs down the spine... feels, not so nice.

What's the trouble? Hold back that scream.
Better to stay hidden... not to be seen.

- the absence of you

The absence of you is sharp, and everywhere I look. The place you used to occupy, is just a grey emptiness now. The stillness is deafening, as my hands busy themselves. I find a strange comfort in All Hallows' eve, or the day of the dead where the line between us is drawn the thinnest. I imagine I can reach out to you, feel your hand stroke my cheek and whisper those old sweet nothings... all those secrets that only one of us now has to keep.

I carve the pumpkin in the same pattern you always did, a crooked smile and triangular eyes. I hang the banners across the doorway, to welcome the trick or treaters. Burdening them with candy apples and sweets, rather than my sadness. I play the music... all the cliche tunes, and dance alone through the empty rooms. I paint over my face with someone's else's character... and by midnight I'm truly alone... wandering in my All Hallows' grieve.

- pale moon witch

Made of porcelain and steel, she is delicate but contains multitudes of strength. She moulds herself to form a pleasing shape, to draw you in... your own mistake. She is the pale moon witch, but it's too late for introductions.

Hair whips from side to side, as her hands spin and turn, conjuring words beyond every day language. Vowels and consonants spew from her mouth in a deadly dance... you stand open mouthed, in a trance. She is the pale moon witch, but it's too late for apologies.

Her eyes are fire and ice intertwined, fiery with orange and yet pale like moonbeams light. She walks above the Earth, and begins her own rebirth. She is the pale moon witch... but it's far too late to save yourself.

- deafening silence

Deafening silence. The spaces between the brick work,
and the draft seeping in. My blood is cold, my skin is
pinched. The ragged moths circle overhead, and the
world is desolate. I ache to take a breath.
I see the flowers. The portrait. I remember.
They remember me.

- tiers for fears

Shout, flout, let your privilege out.

Christmas this year? You'll have to do without.

Come on, we're looking at you, come on... you rule breakers and conformity shakers. You banana bread bakers, and stay at home makers. You clapped and cheered, and now the ugly head of 2020 has reared.

- school announcement

Good morning class,

First of all, those kids who call you fat and ugly and worthless, who crowd around your desk before the teacher walks in... are just a bunch of sheep following a bitchy wolf. The same bitchy wolf who will bump into you in a nightclub when your 18 and apologise for their "mistakes." You may not wear the latest fashions, or have the coolest gadgets, but the friendships your making now will last for decades. Sorry to tell you that your love life will be pretty non-existent until your late teens, and then you will be blown away and torn apart and full of teen angst until your approximately 29. But keep your chin up, it does get better for you. Also, the dread of maths class... well it will never ever EVER be interesting!

Have a good day.

- food love

I lay you bare. Strip away the outer layers, and devour all of you within. Slowly undress and peel back all the nonsense, until the real prize bursts forth... the sizzle and oozing sharpens all my senses.

I run my finger down your centre, caressing and tender. Sweet and sharp all at once, my favourite secret longing... Then I add a cracker, some grapes and the deed is done. I am content and whole again.

- liquor-lipped

Liquor-lipped is a dangerous state. My bitter mouth cannot contain the secrets it usually holds captive. I speak of truth, without the aid of herbs and sleep, the words tumble out of me.

My leaden blood, intoxicated and raw spills all of my resentments onto the bar in front of these strangers. A somber fellow turns to me, says nothing but raises his glass in solidarity to my cause. My inverted heart is crushed with the latest disappointment... I whine about 'how they could do this to me?'

The whisky I consume will not consume my wrath, it flushes my face and fans the flames of my resolve. I must speak with these ghosts... I reach for my phone and start an incoherent sentence to my group of sober idols.

Water would be a calming drink, but I never want to feel sober again.

The joy of drunkenness for me is when I black out... it has the elegance of death without the permanence of committing to it.

I look around, these groups and towers of pint glasses, forced laughs in response to awful chat up lines. I will surpass the rain, and drench my soul with a high percentage bottle of distraction...

- eternity

People seem to think that you only have two options. You can break down, or level up. Celebrate or mourn. So... what to do when age is approaching? The real question... does it matter? No matter what... the time will glide by anyway, so do that thing you've been putting off, make that call, write that letter, set out that intention. You can grow up, or you can grow your soul with all the joy it needs. The child inside never truly goes away, these adults never really know what they're doing. We're made of starlight, eternal and unrelenting, so does an earth age really matter?

- eavesdropping

The world unfolds before me. The weight of words passing softly through the spaces between. Laughter, whispers, anguish, anger, love and mirth. Delicate social etiquette versus abrupt interaction. The inner workings of strangers, whose private lives are vast and deep as drowning in the overwhelming population... my realisations while people watching is that it takes real investment to understand another person, but I'll always end up eavesdropping over a cup of coffee.

- atomic

In-between the waiting, and the not wanting to leave and the anxious wondering... is where hours are kept. The minutes that slip past, race by, drag on, take their toll, take our present and turn it into the past, occupy our future and our worries... that's where the hours live.

The constant movement of a man made structure, as the earth spins in it glorious dance through the cosmos. Seconds, days, years, blend into eternity with no difficulty. They are a grand expanse and a micro verse all in one. The ticking, the sun dial, the calendar, the catalogue of life cycles. The hours spent, are hours we are lent by the universe itself...

... until our atoms spread out again with the stars...

loving

'From where do our hearts grow?
Our mothers, the stem of existence...
or from experience?'

- promises, promises

Promises kept to yourself, have the highest power.

Promises made to loved ones, can change by the hour.

Promises made while rushing,

can crumble and combust.

Promises made in the dark, are influenced by lust.

Promises at sunset, are tinged by blue and gold.

But the one promise I can keep...

is holding you when we are old.

- falling for you

I, stumbling through the darkness, fell and fell and fell... until you shone, showing the safe pathway to tread. And not even starlight could shine as brightly as a smile from your lips... nor fill me with so much wonder. Do not fear the delicate, for many precious things are fragile.

- I am woman

Speak not of cold, for I am fire waiting to be remade. I am the flame and the heat of all those who came before me, I am the warmth and despair, I am the spark that sets off a change. I am the banisher of the cold, I am the remade ember goddess, I am woman.

- youth

Family holidays.

Playground kisses.

Blushing cheeks.

Near misses.

Promised you'd write.

I got one letter.

Parents were right.

Older love was better.

Joys of youth.

Ten year old broken heart.

Had to pick up 10 pieces.

Years later... turn it into art.

- Lily

Small, outstretched and grabbing,
Attention span severely lacking,
Facial expression hidden in hands,
While toes dip in golden sands.

Trotting, crawling, running,
Heartbeats quick and chest thumping,
Dashing, prancing, slowing,
Curling into sleepy moaning.

Trying to tame a bush of curls,
Any beverage liable to spills,
The sound of laughter and distant cries,
This is motherhood, in every size.

- anatomy of a first date

Arrange the muscles in my face to form a pleasant expression, designed to entice you in (and cover up any depression).

Bones crack as I extend my hand, a handshake seems quite normal (maybe we should have hugged... is a handshake far too formal?)

The wine pours into the glass, the conversation flows. The blood rushing around my body, heated, making my skin glow.

You lean forward closer, requesting our first kiss. I close my eyes and hope that our tipsy aim doesn't miss...

- love

Suddenly we're in love. A feeling, an image I never expected to hold in my palm. I trace the outlines of my heart, head and life... as I unfold these secret sentences we whisper to one another... your beauty strikes me, like a brightness I only see in sunlight.

- soulmates

I swallow my happiness in a morning. Quickly, so I don't forget. Happy pills and sunrises go together in my mindset, starting the day as you mean to go onwards. Brightness, alert, blinding light against the creeping darkness as the milligrams wear off from their constant workout. I bathe in the dawn. I soak it in my pores. I crawl back into bed to find you in the tangled sheets. You are my serotonin, your fingertips begin the search for all the places where the sun has kissed me first... and leave your caress upon my chemically altered form. You embrace every shade of my emotional palette. That's the prettiest thing about calling you home... our intertwining souls making their own unique hues, and we can lock the door on the rest of the day's expectations and create our own universe with its own stars.

- embrace

You've put a spell on me. You duped my eyelids into believing realities that can't possibly be true. There is no world where my tenderness is embraced like an old friend, and isn't punished for being too fragile. The cracks in my carefully constructed facade are painted in gold by your careful strokes, and my skin feels bruised within your gentle embrace... feeling undeserving of such care.

- I will wait

Blink into the daylight. Eyes are heavy from broken rest. Throat is sandpaper lined and corse from the words that sliced out the night before. I crawl from the cavernous lonesome morning, into the itching afternoon, into an evening of numbness. I wait for your message. Fingertips tapping as my mind is zapping and my heart is rapping out of my chest. I will wait. I always wait.

- melancholy

An abundance of nesting fowls, this quarry of hunters who seek out the gossip, gather in their flocks to spell it out for one another, to condemn the fire for not being tamed.

I shake the embers, and watch the glow on all the things they told me I could not be. Glasses clinking my success, while sliding down noses to look over my life choices... passions sinking as I move from goal to goal trying to stamp out regrets, and cross off the targets on someone else's list. I suffer from blue melancholy, as I try to paint my own sky like numbers.

- comfort in the darkness

Frosted paths on early morning walks, I wander through an empty land. It cracks my face, a delicate pottery. My expression is winter-sculpted, as I wear last nights broken rest for no-one to witness. I wish that sleep could separate me from my woes, the ink blots stamped into my endless ruminating. We are told not to soothe our souls with medicinal methods, but if I could find the right vintage in spirit... maybe a night cap would anaesthetise me long enough that I could find some comfort in the darkness.

- me

I ache for dreaming.

I long to leave this world behind.

I concentrate deeply in fantasy.

I yearn for the chance to escape.

I cherish the thoughts in my head.

I need distraction and rest.

I hope for the endless nights end.

I desire momentary blissful nothing.

I am a collection of sleepless heads.

I am a collection of fearful dreads.

I am the light and the twisted soul.

I am insomnia... and my tale is told.

- love postponed

Hanging soft and unused
The garment bag zipped tight
The softest satin touch
Seeps out into the night.

Picturing forever,
Yet it never seemed to take so long
My heart is full but heavy
Burdened by our unplayed song.

We had expected
A day we could embrace
Captured in a memory,
Which now we can only chase.

Our love story has to wait
And I am so forlorn
This year has concluded
With our day... being torn.

I imagine all the details,
The flowers in the sky
Our eyes interlocking,
In sweet soft sighs.

We hope for tomorrow,
The anticipation makes me ache.
The waiting and the wondering...
All for our loves sake...

- oh love

Oh love,

There is nothing more beautiful in this world,

Than the curve of your lips

When you look into my soul

And say everything... without sound or reason.

Yet your mouth, irresistible, haunts me.

It's in the outline of all my dreams and fantasies.

Calling me home... calling me to abandonment

and wanting.

- to me, from me

Tonight's the night, to dress the eve. Swathes of swaying holly trees. The ringing out of distant bells, clear your throats for the carol of hells.

Those January resolutions mean farewell to fruitcake and cheese platters, and naughty nightmares that size matters. Well how about this new year... we give ourselves a break? Who cares about all the things we bake, or even which resolutions we do (or do not) make?

Instead of simply dreaming of pine, let's still pretend it's Christmas time. Let's stun the elves, and give a Christmas present to ourselves.

Throw out our worries, our expectations and nervous flurries. Enjoy the year for all it could bring, rejoice in the new and laugh and sing.

- the inked darkness

Dreams strike me, like a wave upon a shore. I spend long nights staring into the inked darkness, that I rarely notice when I sink into unconsciousness. Sweet memories contorted with painful worries into strange landscapes. A sunset across a vast ocean reflects like a bleeding shore. Red stained sand on bleached coral cheeks... pale daylight wakes me, disorientation distorts my morning call.

- bloom

The smell that comes after pouring rain...
that fresh peace, that cleansing of the soul, the sweet
fragrance of storms... what my mind searches for daily.

I stare through glass at the copper-toned eve of a day
ending, look across the field at the swaying grass...
imagine the endless crops of peace settling for the night,
with their silent roots keeping firm grip on our spinning
world.

I return from my wandering eyes, to hear the noise in
the walls, the neighbours back and forth dialogue of
domestic requests.

My door opens, he returns to me with common place
blooms... the bouquets he buys for love and not only for
an occasion, or for guilt. Guilty blooms lack the depth of
feeling, but his blooms always illuminate my darkness.

- madre

A vision in my mind
Motherhood contrived
Social media perfection
Images collection

Artist impression
5 minutes a session
Individual perception
The human condition.

Spend the day scrolling
Disengage from the trolling
The burden of modern
Keeps our emotions sodden.

Strive for some kindness
Leave the hate behind us
We hope to be better
As we envy each captioned letter.

\- mama

The question lingers
Am I mad or a mother?
Better take a test.

- undecided

My garments say "she's undecided." Hasn't settled on a theme for her life. Some days my uniform is all black (slimming allegedly... no expectations).

Other days it's rainbows and too many patterns at the same time. Blaring, distracting and boisterous. T-shirts with witty slogans, dungarees and socks covered in cute animals. Such a Gemini... I wear that emblem round my neck, so people know my "type." 2 personalities, 2 sides of the same coin.

The outfit I wear most often is motherhood. Whatever is closest, easiest and clean! The moment I step through my front door, I climb eagerly into my pjs. Comfy, dependable, another variety of textures and colours to account for my mood swings.

- festive lullaby

A kiss of coal, as soot escapes onto the fireplace. This indoor shower, much warmer than the icy bower under which we walk on winter days. The frozen muddled path, stained by the bright splashes of holly. A distant memory whilst watching the flames dance in the darkness.

What ails the angels who sing their nightly chorus in our dreaming minds? Is it the frosty fowls, their resting place a kitchen table to be prepared for feasts? Freckled with light from twinkling stars adorning every corner of our haven. It is a candy cane curse, to be so happy and so retched all at once.

The sweetness of the season, mixed with the poison of expectation, experience and those chimney fumes. The haunted holiday, where we feel absence all the more from the loved ones we have lost and still adore. We crave good thoughts and mulled cider to raise toasts to those memories.

We light the spirits candle, to throw our arms around the ghosts on holiday. Under star filled nights, we roll enormous snow balls to make them anew... in the figure of snowmen, named with snowman's letters spelt out with those pieces of coal. We hang our weathered stockings up to dry, and sing to the eve a sweet lullaby...

- nerd sanctuary

Whirring of an Xbox fan, as other half muttering under his breath goes wandering on missions for a clan. Balls of every coloured wool lay next to me, as I twist and turn... letting another new pom pom burst free. Lamp light flickering in the corner, no flame... just old, getting warmer. Rows and rows of blu-rays, discs can take us on new adventures on any of the days. Inevitably we end up re-watching friends, laughing at all the same jokes and cry at all the same ends. The walls are magnolia and plain, but artwork hangs up and signed with a friends name. Date night we might add wine and a scented candle, close the door quietly and expertly lock the handle. The second hand furniture (lived in) is a mish mash of gifted pieces, as our lives together grow and modern love increases.

- mind boxes

I stare at the tatty and torn exterior, hiding inner depths. I slowly peel back the tape, and find snapshots of my childhood. Running on all fours pretending to be a big cat, fish fingers for tea, singing 'Lion King' songs in the school talent show... pushing, shoving, crying, crying out for acceptance. Piles of scripts from plays and musicals and sketches and drama clubs. Failed auditions for parts, for a place in friendship groups, for childhood crushes.

I rip off the next boxes tape... quick and painless... to expose the ghosts of relationships past. The literal ghosting, the "it's not you it's me," the "I don't want a relationship right now, or at least not with you." The bruises, the scars, the stitches. The lies, the arguing, the hours of tears and regret. The mistakes, the betrayals of friendship lost.

The last box I'm more gentle with. Train tickets for our first date, a drunken selfie before I caught the last train home, a million text messages. Cinema tickets, theatre stubs and hospital wristbands from the week I spent trying to coax out a child. Delicate and precious and all encompassing love.

- my muse

I hoard my adolescent experiences. Birthday cards, my first love letter, the first pair of glasses I ever wore. I collect pieces of handwriting, some of the loops and swirls made by souls long since passed. I keep a firm grip on all the things my mind one day might let wander off, so I can carefully tend to my muse long after I forget their mannerisms. I write you, like these shoebox memories, methodically but passionately, crafting every word like each letter is on a potters wheel. I spin out of control, but I keep my little world out of the disarray of the sticky hands of public viewing.

- happy place

Where sea meets sky, the sand curves into a smile.
Rock rises from the water, small islands and small
worlds filled with sea life. A path leads down to the
softest of sand, covered in shells and family memories.
The air is fresh and salty and alive.

- thank you

So many thanks are needed,
For the way you always believed.
You gave me the courage to grow,
Helped me to step back and breathe.

Always so patient and kind,
Understanding... and wonderfully weird.
We belly laugh in the dark,
And you grow a beautiful beard!

You have faith in my whims and my ways,
One of my biggest supporters.
You have brightened up all of my days,
And created two beautiful daughters.

- the truth

Drink away the long hours, and gut all the flowers...

to give true love the stalks.

Because all petals wilt, but real love is built

on the truth of the deep dark talks.

- bittersweet

Our Sun gives us warmth, a glowing sight. Head and
heart, locked in bitterest fight. Fate is sealed by the
lines on your skin... and life is what happens,
when you let it all in.

- beginnings

The invitation gathers dust. The swirling turning calligraphy of faded hearts, and old dates and times. The bottled former excitement tastes like stale champagne, the fizz has gone out of all our former plans. And the kiss that we so highly anticipated, is now the kiss that never comes... it doesn't taste the same way. We have paused, slowed down, pondered how we got to this point in time. We gather our resolve, lift the pen to paper, and sketch out a new plan. A new start to our new start together...

- spectre

"The streets are slick, cold and wet.

Unaffected currently, as I watch seated inside.

This is an unfamiliar landscape to me, these shop fronts and endless doorways. Not the streets I grew up walking on.

'Outsider', I feel like they whisper behind the counter when they take my order for tea or cake. I order something to give me a right to be taking up space here. Sitting alone in a cafe, with this teapot as my crutch. I pour myself a large measure of camomile.

Nothing matches here. The teapot a pale grey, similar to the shade of an unwashed net hanging in the front window. The cup is bone China, with delicate pink flowers, and the plate has a harsh outline of dull green leaves. I easily can relate to curvy jagged edges.

People staring in as they walk the high street... I feel like a fair ground goldfish in a new bowl. Out of my natural territory, enclosed, caged. The solitary swimmer, eating quietly as the world swirls around my head. Orders that need completing, and gossip to be passed on.

The yellow sugar bowls with the silver tongs rattle whenever the front door opens. The clang of the bell to announce a new arrival. I always look up although I'm not expecting company. My table of 4 has 3 empty chairs, so I place my bag on one as though to save a seat for a transparent companion.

The breeze shakes the bunting above my head. Floral and cream coloured, hanging over shelves with rows of loose leaf tea for sale. This world hustles and bustles, but I am a constant. Unmoving and unmoved, other than occasionally turning a page in my book so I look relaxed.

When I left my old haunt, the one that had haunted me... I left a lifetime behind with it.
Came to these greener, grey pastures. Became an unfamiliar face in new gingham clothed surroundings, but the anxiety I tried to hide myself from stalked me regardless. It still recognised my face.

There are miles between the past and this present. Yet I have no presence. Conversations continue on around me, and without me. I'm a spectre in the corner of the room, the human equivalent of that mismatched teapot."

- grandad

"The weight of lost memories,
as I held you paper thin."

- a vacant space

It stood in the corner of the room, next to the vast multi panelled window. It crisscrossed in a diamond formation, like the lattice on top of an apple strudel. Old memories of his cooking surface... his large hands working multiple hobs at once in a warm kitchen, plus an oven and a microwave. In several places at once but his mind focused, like a laser beam, concentrating on several tasks all at one time while joining in the conversation in the next room, throwing in a joke like the salt he'd snuck into the pan. That was his chair.

Like himself really... soft warm and inviting. Comfortable and reliable, a little worn and old but still more than capable of caring for a person's comfort. We tried to keep him comfortable towards the end. He didn't leave the chair very much during those years. The arms grew weathered, like the skin on his hands which had once been so busy. The comfort began to look like restraints... keeping him against his will.

- yours

Capture the light falling across your face...
hold it gently in my palm, cupped in a sweet embrace.

Breathless endless times, of days and nights intwined.
Regardless of time, of season, of year...
I will always be yours, and always hold you dear.

Age will not erase the kindness you always show,
even if the present subtly suddenly...
becomes the past of long long ago.

- seasonal

As the clock hands slip forward, summer time skips along. The new day dawns more quickly, pink with the topcoat of summer song. Birds stretch out their chorus, as they chatter and they sing. They skip from new leaf to new leaf, that were cradled softly in the spring. Autumn will always have my heart, winter time is cosy, but spring and summer bring the softness of a posie.

growing

'Do not fear the delicate,
for many precious things are fragile.'

- triad

There were three.
And these three were doors.
Each door had a name.
A name unspoken in years.

Gilded golden edges.
Edges trimmed in sunlight.
Sunlight stripping shadows bare.
Shadows left by twilight hours.

These names were ordered.
Ordered by significance.
Significance to our nature.
But nature has lost its power to speak.

These long forgotten doors.
Forgotten in dusty memories.
Dusty memories of a journey.
A journey to the oldest land.

Each contained a reflection.
A reflection of surprised expression.
Expression of wonder and truth.
The truth contained and mirrored.

- nikki and the millions

My prison.
Not a place, a time, a crime.
Not a ceiling, a meaning, a feeling.
My bodily prison holds me captive.

Shuttered in existence,
Lifetime of resistance,
Advice littering empty space.
While you get to leave, I stay in place.

Jailed, yet I'm a victim.
Thief in the night, in the day.
You steal my time...
Lead my mind astray.

I detest my lonely island.
This barren world I hold.
Burning, aching, turning..
Listless, hopeless, yearning.

Request and invites stop,
As I stare down the clock.
Years spent reminiscing...
By the millions who are missing.

- 'prosemotional honesty'

If we're entirely honest with ourselves,
Emotions are a fickle mysterious beast.

We all claim to be seeking out a quiet life. Lacking in drama or conflict or confrontation.

Truth be told, many of us crave just that.
The ache of feeling left out, gives us an engaging topic to talk about.

We complain, and moan, and judge, and are baffled. We sigh and rage and ponder, all the while there is a quiet satisfaction laid deep in our chests, as we have a conversation starter.

Our words escape from our mouths, full of vinegar and salted. Spitting and jerking with condemnation at this offence. The expected reaction and all part of the pretence.

A third glass of wine rambled dissection of the human condition, theories as to how we ended up in such a predicament. Suggestions of strategies and battle plans of how to deal with this complicated completely unjustified melancholy.

We place down our evidence, piece by piece, creating a timeline of our own goodness and deeds. Our enabler in this discussion, leaning forward and nodding, their agreement gives us justification to order the fourth and burst forth with all the knowledge we'd kept hidden... because we are a good person.

- queens

There's a certain pride in private growth. Making dreams come true quietly, observing how that makes you feel. Do you really need praise from anyone other than your own mind? Do you set goals for yourself, or from outside expectations? Make art, make a mess, make it your own way, make it about you for once and not about those 'so- called' opinions. You are a queen, a warrior, a visionary, a masterpiece, an ever-growing ever changing goddess. There's a certain pride in looking at your reflection, and feeling whole on your own terms.

- what I will miss about summer...

I will miss spontaneous activity. Day-drinking, bbq's with friends, date nights to the cinema, sitting outdoors watching the sunset slowly over the horizon.

I will miss the landscape. Wild flowers, bees hovering over pollen (which I will take anti-histamines to compensate for!) Rambles through long grass and sunlight drifting through bright green canopies.

I will miss freedom. Quality time, hugs and kisses, sharing warmth and memories with family. I will miss the 'old normalcy' during the summer of 2020... but autumn is my true calling. It's blanket covered nights, filled with candle light laughter and hot drinks will be my revival and our rebirth, nature's endless cycle.

- the steadiest of seasons

I turn my eyes heaven ward. Staring into the velvet blackness with the smallest pin pricks of hope.

O' lustful moon, you smile down upon me, tempt me to a place beyond this world I'm sunken into. Clasping the autumn wine in my hand... I drain it dry and place the crystal patterned comfort by my side.

The breeze stirs the doting trees, who are keeping careful watch over my despair. My brazen desire to escape, but with no path laid out before me... no clear direction or compass can guide me. Autumn is the steadiest of the seasons... we are all well acquainted with loss. Leaves curl and fall from their birth place, it's the way of the natural order. I close my eyes, and bathe my thoughts in the will to become that leaf. Drifting on the wind, and freedom.

- conjured

Swirling, tumbling, turning.

Quick hands, and swift churning.

The sombre quiet without an ear to hear it.

Bland darkness scattered by pinpricks of fire.

Breathless, porcelain shattered.

Skin illuminated by deepest blue.

Ocean spray flays me bare.

Ancient bones broken over rocks.

Bleached... without care.

- follow the footsteps

Follow the winter footsteps, tumbling into the glistening morning dew. See those delicate feet, turn toward the dawn of springtime.

Listen to the bluebells chime, ringing their sweet melodic sound. The pale fresh snowdrops, stand against newly patterned diamonds of snowfall.

The lightest flutters of a breeze, with stilled greenery on frosted landscape. The transparent wings unfurling, quickly take their flight.

Into this new day, closing out the navy blue of night passed. A golden shining shimmers, gleaming with all the impossible.

This slightest touch of magic weaves it's way on by.
A sprinkling of fresh dandelion seeds, with their gentle feathered tops.

As the sun peeks softly through the treetops, and illuminates this new world. There is a hush, before the birds chorus.

Those tiny hands of delicate digits, clamouring up barren stalks still waiting to bloom anew. They quickly search with glittering eyes, for the perfect solitary spot.

Gaze rests on brightest splashes of forget me not, where they'll leave behind sweet memories....

- growing up

Does anyone ever grow up?

As a child, I felt like adults were these all knowing beings who always knew what to do in any situation. They would protect me, they would guide me, they would steer me to my future with care. Infallible, omniscient creatures full of wise words, council and weighty opinions.

The truth of adulthood... is that we are all large children with no clue what we're doing!

When did I know I had "grown up?" When I stopped trying to prove it to everyone else.

- beginnings

All this waiting, will eventually lead to the best days of your life. Hand holding, wide open spaces filled up with warm embraces. Hellos said in person, not on another video chat. Crossing over thresholds, wiping boots on a different greeting mat. As I hold each of you close to my heart, after this cold dark emptiness of spending life apart... all this sacrifice, will eventually lead to a new joyful beginning.

- mirror, mirror

The mirror doesn't see my loyalty.

The way my finger tips trace my lovers skin.

The times I cry at some poorly constructed rom-com plot line. My concentration face as I read an untold tale.

How a piece of music moves me and through me so gently and violently all at once.

The mirror doesn't see my inner beauty, it just shows all the flaws I wish I could forget.

- renewal

Renewal, growth, expansion.

Tentative life coiled and encased throughout the harsh

cold, springs forth, finally begins to unfurl.

Reaching, grasping for solid foundations.

Mind your step in spring, for you may step on

something precious, and irrevocably change its course.

- inevitable entropy

There are three things of which we can be certain.
My chest blooms, expands, contracts when I think too
deeply about any of them.
We are lucky and doomed to experience them all.
We are the living, the loving, and the dying,
all at once.

- flaws

- My bullet points have bullet points.
- I'm an overachiever when it comes to lists and planning. I write and re-write until the day of an event. I dedicate so much thought to my relationships. Have I communicated recently, have I asked about the other person, have I shown an interest in things that are important to them. I become fixated on new projects, and obsess over every detail. My anxious tendencies make me empathetic and deeply concerned for others and our world. I like to send thankyou cards and painstakingly try to find suitable gifts months in advance. I'll eat toast in favour of someone else having a lavish meal of their choice. I tidy my spaces because I cannot tidy my mind. Organising programmes are my therapy and comfort. Seeing the little rainbows in a drawer of pens, does more for my soul than an hour of unburdening myself, and it's guilt free! When I laugh I just let it go. My belly shakes and my mouth is wide, and people seem to appreciate the affect their humours had on me.

- cocoon

Crunchy leaves in sweet autumn breeze.

Swirls of yellow, dance across my path.

Breath curls from my lips, hidden under tightly wrapped knitted necks.

Steam rises from patterned mugs, filled with chocolate, cream and sprinkled cocoa. Blankets heaped upon pyjama clothed laps, candles flicker with mellow season scents.

Tired bodies sink into softest furnishings, while autumnal sleep wraps us in the most gentle cocoon.

- the fall

I wear my moods like the seasons, but my favourite past-time is autumn living. I live for knitwear covered skin, my longest scarf in the hues of orange and red trailing across the ground I trace my steps in. My cheeks blush within the crisp cool air, and the smell of freshly brewed tea lingers in my hair long after it's finished. I cradle my hands inside mittens which keep my darkest secrets hidden inside the early evening sunsets. Spring renews my spirit after a dark night, and I can pick the dandelions for my honey jars. Summer gives lazy long afternoon conversations. Winter has the bite and edges of waiting for a lover to come home who you dearly miss. None of these feel like home to me, in the way that autumn holds my heart close.

- forest

Let me wander through cascading branches.
The wind twists and turns the world I'm under.
Creatures of the wildness run across my path.
Seeking nurturing life, with foraging heartbeats.

Skip through the carpet of shining wet leaves.
Acorns scattered like celebratory confetti.
The season of change has opened its door,
And I breathe in the taste of the land.

The palette of the sky stretches before me.
Fog lifts to the sight of duck egg blue.
I reach out my hand to feel damp bark,
And although alone... I'm not in my heart.

- festive necessities

Snuggled under my warm winter sheets.

Grey with white patterns of stags and woodland creatures... protection from the outside world of the grey winter skies.

Legs already covered in holiday bruises from slipping on the icy path, skidding to my knees as though in a compulsive prayer... stared at by the passers by, questioning eyes under cloth masks.

These are the habits of frost, beauty and pain intertwined. Lovely to observe, yet bitter to experience first hand (or knee). I line my evergreen pockets with receipts of all those festive necessities, the cold remedies and pick me ups. I line my bed with my own body, slinking into the warm spot he leaves for me... nestled and stillness.

- being human

I wake bleary eyed and forlorn, ripped away from the comfort of temporary nothingness... I pull on my human suit, my muscles forming a smile, my hands crafting the new day. I assume graces bones, I crack and stretch, I walk in expectation of what I might encounter in a new months toil. I scroll the device like a morning bulletin, see the bliss of your name, the late or early message before you closed your eyes to the upcoming day light. He provokes the night, walking through the darkness and the cold of a January wind, completing a check list of tasks before climbing into the crease I left behind, that my body heat used to occupy.

- drink the stars

With destitute hearts, we look to the sky. Lonely eyes searching. Kept apart by design, we hope that those other distanced eyes are watching the same vale of stars we are. That if they can see the universe the same way we do, that will bring them one step closer to our arms. Joining hands together in a far off place, in a warm embrace, like joining cold hands with the sun. Forget the pain, the emptiness, the longing... forget this moon and drink the stars in together... under the same velvet night.

- shaping the world

I am in shape.

I want to shape the world with my writers hands. Carve my name in the bedrock of history, leave my footprints on a desolate island of earth. Evidence we were here at all. Every civilisation has fallen, why not ours? Embrace the green art of opportunity laid out like a welcome matt of the future.

- I no longer worry about...

Fomo or the fear of missing out. I don't need to worry that by staying at home everyone or everything is having a far better time without me being there, or that I've ruined anyone's fun by turning up in the first place, because no-ones making plans! I don't have to check in advance who will be attending, what the timeline will be or even what food will be served to brace myself. My social life is now FaceTime appointments and people seem eager to catch up...

Wedding planning stress. The likelihood I will get married in 2020 is rapidly ebbing away like steam escaping the kettle im constantly boiling. There's no longer a need for that long tearful conversation about what to dress people in, or what will they really be saying about us behind our backs during the whole day. Everybody will (potentially) be at home.

News bulletins. The times of day that would normally have me flicking over the channel as fast as possible, because my brain couldn't focus on so much pain all at once. That pain has been condensed into one panicked 2 hour session of PM updates followed by the 6pm news, at which point I flee to the bathroom for a long quiet soak away from the rest of humanity. I no longer need feel guilty about this bath either, as my body desperately requires some comfort after the onslaught of statistics and predictions.

My children's future, my own future and the planets future. Before this, eco-anxiety was at the forefront of my brain. All day every day it creeped in, the terror of what might be. Terror is now fixed on coughs and colds and 'what ifs'. But the bright spots of my day are the stories of nature healing... the people who can see blue skies without pollution for the first time in their lives. But that is why I kiss them 50 times a day, and tell them I love them at every opportunity, and do our best as a family to be present, because the present is all we are promised...

We've proved we can change. The power that consumerism and "lifestyle choice" and economy had over us all, has been smashed to pieces. And despite my new anxiety for my families health... I feel a glimmer of hope for the health of our planet. It's healing without our interference, as we stay safely in our constructed boxes. The power we rely on now comes from our health service and the tireless efforts of those front line people... I will anxiously hope for each and everyone of your safe returns to your bed.

- the sun & the moon

We sit together, legs crossed over grass, waiting for the moonrise. The sun and moon cross over one another, like old friends passing in the street. A nod of the head before continuing on their separate ways. Lives running parallel but never quite in sync with the other. The worms creep out while the birds are sleeping, freedom in the cool night air away from the earths warmth. Beneath this cold moon, we sit together. Legs crossed over grass, hands crossed over each other, gentle breeze passing over us. The summer doesn't seem to have much silence, but summer evenings have such bliss. The caress of time spent over the sun, and time spent under the moonlight illuminates our lives.

- to my dear ones,

I hope to leave you a better world than the news reports I had to navigate, with the daily worries for what might come. I hope the air in your lungs is clean, as is the water in your oceans. That you can deeply breathe sighs of relief and gratitude, because we changed our ways for you. My only wish is for you to happily... exist.

My loves, I leave you in the knowledge that you made me feel entirely and completely loved, in all of our days together. Nothing has felt more like home to me than you... even when you sleep roll onto me at 3am. I look at you in the dark, and there is light.

- & to myself

For the rest of your days, be kinder. Be kinder to your fragile heart, the one who worries so intensely after every interaction, replays every word and look of a conversation. Has to count to 10 to calm the dread that creeps in. Has to remind you to breathe. The world is a scary place, but there is beauty and love and kindness and that is worth everything.

acknowledgements

Jamie, I couldn't do any of this without you. Our partnership, the unconditional love and strength you give me every single day... completely changed my world for the better. You gave me the gift of motherhood (in two ways!), a muse for my happy scribbles, and I absolutely adore you and our beautiful girls with all of my heart. F&A.

Thank-you to both of our families for being there for us, loving us, supporting us and being a brilliant bunch of humans we are so grateful for, and love immeasurably. Special mentions to my Mum and Dad and Nannan Joan for investing in this project and helping me to make it a reality. Also to my sister Nikki, for inspiring my poem about ME awareness/inspiring me as a person. Deb and Neil and Ann for being the 'wranglers' of an amazing bunch of in-laws that I can't imagine life without now.

To our friends... The Old School/Theatre Gang & Partners... the value of true lasting friendships is priceless. We've been through a lot together over the years, and I appreciate all the adventures we've had and continue to have, and of course the ridiculous group chat memes, endless zoom quizzes and a lot of laughter and love!

Special mentions to Carla, Helen, Emily and Nick and Mel at 'The Rabbit Hole' Bookshop in Brigg, who have shown me such kindness and support on this new journey and have received many anxious messages from me!

Many thanks to Partnership Publishing/Daisa Publishing for all your enthusiasm about my words, all of the hard work and dedication you've put in and coping with my many emails/many notes!

Also thanks to the lovely writers, poets and authors I've virtually met courtesy of zoom/social media, who've really inspired me with my own writing and have given me the courage to finally... just let go, and put myself out there.